whisky
cocktails

whisky
cocktails

david biggs

NEW
HOLLAND

First published in 2009 by New Holland Publishers (UK) Ltd
London • Cape Town • Sydney • Auckland

Garfield House
86–88 Edgware Rd
London W2 2EA
United Kingdom

80 McKenzie Street
Cape Town 8001
South Africa

Unit 1
66 Gibbes Street
Chatswood
NSW 2067
Australia

218 Lake Road
Northcote
Auckland
New Zealand

ISBN 978 1 84773 286 6

Commissioning editor Clare Sayer
Designer Sue Rose
Photographer Ian Garlick
Recipe stylist Nicki Gee
Production Marion Storz
Editorial direction Rosemary Wilkinson

1 3 5 7 9 10 8 6 4 2

Reproduction by Pica Digital Pte Ltd, Singapore
Printed and bound by Tien Wah Press (Pte) Ltd, Malaysia

contents

introduction

> I like to have a martini,
> Two at the very most –
> Three and I'm under the table,
> Four and I'm under the host.

Dorothy Parker

This little book is not intended to be a comprehensive guide to whisky in all its subtle variations. It's a light-hearted look at some of the aspects of this versatile liquor, with a drop of history and a splash of fun thrown in, and a shaker of recipes to tease the purist's palate. So pour yourself a chapter, sit back and sip it just for fun.

From our earliest history, wherever civilisations have been established, alcoholic drinks have been made and enjoyed.

The ancient Egyptians made beer and wine, the Greeks and Romans enjoyed fine wines. Primitive African tribes made beer from sorghum grain and a powerful drink from the fermented berries of the Marula tree. Desert tribes in the Middle East made an alcoholic drink by fermenting mare's milk, and in early South American civilizations cactus and aloe juice were used to create intoxicating beverages.

Most of the early civilisations worshipped a god of drinking, which shows the high esteem in which alcohol was held. Nobody bothered about a god of eating. Bacchus (or Dionysus, if you were Greek) was probably the most popular of the ancient gods, and in modern times St Vincent of Saragossa is regarded as the patron saint of wine and vinegar makers by the Catholic Church. His annual name day is celebrated in all civilised countries where wine is produced. In many religions, ancient and modern, wine still plays an important role in solemn ceremonies. Alcohol, it seems is still regarded with reverence.

The form that the various alcoholic drinks assumed was simply a matter of which ingredients were available in the area. The warm regions of Italy and France were ideal for growing grapes, so wine became the drink of the Mediterranean lands. In the cold and misty regions of Ireland and Scotland grapes simply didn't survive, but barley and other grains did. It was not long before the canny Celts worked out how to turn this natural resource into a brew that quenched the thirst and raised the spirits.

It's not a very difficult thing to make an alcoholic drink. Fermentation is a natural process by which yeasts react with sugars to make alcohol and carbon dioxide gas. Yeasts and sugars occur naturally in many plants, so the first alcoholic drinks probably made themselves and were discovered by happy accident. Perhaps some ripe berries dropped into a rock pool where they were crushed by a passing mammoth and then warmed by the sun until the yeast spores on their skins reacted with the sugar inside. By and by a thirsty and angry cave man returned from his unsuccessful hunt and knelt down to drink the sweet juice in the pool, and suddenly the world seemed a much happier place. He became less angry about the deer that had escaped his arrow and realised his woman was more beautiful than she had ever been.

For thousands of years beer and wine – in their various forms – have helped to keep the human race happy, softening our disappointments and increasing our passions.

Alcohol is a magnifier of emotions. It makes lovers more amorous and fighters more aggressive. It was issued to sailors in the days of sailing ships, to give them courage before climbing the storm-lashed rigging to splice the broken mainbrace. It makes happy people more joyful and sad people much more miserable. This is why it is never wise to try to drown your sorrows. Sorrows are excellent swimmers.

The introduction of distillation raised the whole matter of drinking to a new and more exciting level. (The art of distillation was actually known more than 5000 years ago in ancient Egypt, where it was used to produce perfumes for elegant ladies. Indeed, the word 'alcohol' is said to have come from the Arabic al-kohl, with kohl being the dark powder used as eye make-up.) Distillation of alcoholic drinks began in about the twelfth century and spread rapidly through Europe to Ireland and Scotland. There, instead of having a little alcohol wafting about peacefully in a glass of beer or wine, it leapt out of the container in its pure form to become the forerunner of modern brandy and whisky.

The first distillers were so excited they called it the Water of Life (Eau de Vie) as some believed it would give the drinker eternal youth. It dissolved inhibitions and made quite dull people feel that they were incredibly clever. Distillers have been refining it ever since. And dull people have been enjoying their instant wisdom.

The first whiskey was distilled in Ireland, and the loyal Irish claim it was introduced by St Patrick himself. It was called, in the Celtic language, 'Uisge Beatha', the Water of Life. This was shortened to Usquebaugh and later to Uisky. The English, who have always felt they knew better and couldn't pronounce 'uisge beatha' properly anyway, pronounced it 'whiskey'.

This magical Water of Life was said to cure almost any pain and was first used as a medicine. This is not surprising. Alcohol is a powerful disinfectant and wine has recently been found to possess medicinal properties.

No matter what the basic ingredients are, the production of spirit drinks is a two-stage process. The first stage consists of fermentation, in which the sugar and yeast combine to create a substance that includes alcohol. It may be a basic wine or beer or fermented aloe juice (as in tequila) or the crushed and fermented juice of sugar cane (as in rum). The second stage is distillation, in which the alcohol is removed from the fermented beverage, condensed and collected.

Alcohol, as it drips straight from the still, is not a particularly palatable drink. Before it can be enjoyed it must be softened by diluting it. Most whiskies are bottled at around 40% alcohol by volume. Stronger than this and the result is a fiery liquid that sears the palate so badly that you can taste hardly any actual flavour at all. The distilled product is often matured in oak casks for many years to add flavour and smoothness.

The end product, whether it is gin, brandy, rum or whisky, is the result of years of experience in blending and maturing the spirit to achieve its distinctive flavour. While all whiskies are made in basically the same way, there are many hundreds of individual brands on the market, each with its own character and each the result of a particular distiller and blender's skill and style.

The earliest written reference to whisky is found in a document from the Scottish Exchequer Rolls in 1494. It records the sale of 'Eight bolls of malt to Friar John Cor wherewith to make aquavitae.' The first liquor tax was introduced in 1644, when King Charles First of England became worried that there would be a shortage of cereals for food, following a poor harvest. He imposed a tax on the Water of Life, setting a nasty precedent which has lasted to this day. Wherever they are produced, alcoholic drinks provide government with a very lucrative source of revenue. This is a two-edged sword because, no matter how much a puritan government may disapprove of liquor consumption, they still enjoy the revenue it generates.

how it's made

> Actually, it only takes one drink to get me drunk. The trouble is I can never remember whether it's the thirteenth or the fourteenth.

George Burns

Traditionally, the distilled product from Scotland is called 'whisky', while that made in other countries is usually spelled 'whiskey' with the 'e'. The exception is Canada, where they make whisky without an 'e'. Only the very finest palates claim to be able to taste that 'e'.

Many books have been written about the fine art of distilling and blending, and if the reader wishes to learn more it should not be difficult. The following is a highly simplified description of the way whisky is made.

The first stage in the making of good whisky is the creation of malt.

To do this the grain (usually barley) is steeped in water until it germinates. When this happens and the cereal starts to sprout, the seeds excrete an enzyme which converts the starch into sugar. Many health fanatics use sprouted grain or beans in salads, which they claim are full of goodness.

They probably are, too.

The sprouted grain is then spread out on malting floors, where it is dried to stop the sprouting process, and allowed to 'cure' for up to two weeks, during which time it is turned constantly. Drying is

above: Checking barley grains for sprouting

often achieved by burning peat below the malted grins. This is done for two reasons. The heat stops the sprouting and the fragrant blue smoke adds a characteristic peaty character to the flavour.

Once cured, the sprouted grain is sifted to remove the rootlets and shoots and it is placed in hot water to form a runny 'mash' rather like thin porridge. This converts any remaining starch into sugar and the liquid is drained off to form a kind of simple beer, or 'wort'. The solid matter that remains is sold as animal feed while yeast is added to the wort to start the fermentation process.

After fermentation the 'wash' will have an alcohol content of around 7% by volume (slightly more than regular beer or ale).

So far the process has been similar to that of brewing beer. At this stage, however, whisky-making takes a new direction – distillation.

Alcohol boils at a lower temperature than water, so when the fermented grain liquor is placed in an enclosed container and heated, the alcohol evaporates first and is collected in a condenser, which cools it and turns it back from vapour to the liquid that will eventually become whisky.

The finest whiskies are made in large, onion-shaped copper containers called 'pot-stills'. This is a costly and labour-intensive business because each batch is distilled separately, then the still must be emptied, cleaned and re-filled for the next batch. A faster method uses the more modern continuous still, in which the wort passes over superheated steam and a continuous stream of alcohol results. This rather characterless alcohol is sometimes used in blended whiskies to increase volume and reduce the cost.

Although Scotland is probably the best known whisky producing country, the Irish were the first to create the drink, and many connoisseurs still consider Irish Whiskey to be the pinnacle of perfection.

One difference between the Scots and Irish products is that the Scots distil their mash twice, while the Irish do it three times.

Another difference is that the Scots make theirs entirely from malted barley, while the Irish often use a blend of malted and unmalted grain, sometimes with wheat and rye added to the blend. (The rest of the world is free to make whiskey by any method they choose.)

After distillation the liquor has an alcohol content of around 80% by volume and is colourless and rather characterless. Before becoming proper whisky it must be matured and blended to add individuality and flavour. It must also be brought down to a more manageable alcohol level of around 40% by volume.

Most whisky-producing countries have laws that make it compulsory for the distilled liquor to be stored in oak barrels for at least three years. In most cases Scotch and Irish whiskies are kept in casks for far longer than the statutory three years. The barrels that are used

below: Scottish whisky barrels being stored in a cellar

sometimes held sherry or some other liquor before being put into service in the whisky cellars, and the flavour is leeched out by the alcohol to add to the complexity of the whisky. This, of course, plays an important role in the final flavour of the product. Casks that were previously used for Sherry will impart a different flavour to Madeira barrels.

Experienced blenders taste the product of each barrel and select those they know will harmonise to create the exact flavour they require.

From the location of the peat and the water used in the making of whisky, to the malting of the grain, the selection of barrels and the blending and maturation, every stage contributes to the individuality of the end product. The variations are endless, which is why whiskies – and whiskeys – come in an almost infinite range of flavours and styles.

Enthusiastic collectors of Scotch whiskies often accumulate huge numbers of different ones and it is not unusual to find a private cellar containing more than 200 single malts. It's worth tasting as many as you can, because sooner or later you'll find the one that is perfectly suited to your palate.

The age indicated on a bottle of whisky denotes the number of years the whisky was kept in casks. Once it has been bottled it does not age further. A whisky blend often contains malts of various ages and the age that is given is always that of the youngest component of the blend.

Tasting

It has become a standard joke among non wine-drinkers to mock the antics of professional wine tasters. All that swirling, sniffing, rolling of eyes and spitting is just asking to be parodied. To the outsider, whisky tasting appears to be a rather more dignified process.

The technique for tasting whiskies is slightly different from that of tasting wine, although things like 'nose', 'palate' and 'mouth-feel' are equally important.

Most of what we think of as 'taste' is actually a combination of aromas and flavours. Like wine, whisky is described in terms of colour, body, fullness, depth and finish (which is the lingering after-taste).

Distilled drinks, with their high alcohol content, are highly volatile and release their aromas far more readily than wines, which have a comparatively low alcohol content. (Most wines have alcohol levels between 10 and 15% by volume.) For this reason whisky is not swirled around in the glass, as wine is. It is simply held under the nose and sniffed. The whisky taster doesn't stick his or her nose right into the glass, either, as wine tasters do. If they did they'd get an overpowering lung-full of spirit vapour and probably lose their breath for a few moments. (In a good whisky that first gentle sniff will probably reveal a distinctively smoky aroma of peat.)

Also, unlike wine, the flavour is not enhanced by swishing it about in the mouth. It is simply held there while the layers of complex flavour unfold. In the mouth it should feel smooth and not harsh or burning. It should not taste bitter. Think of terms like silky, warm, rich, smoky, velvety and smooth.

After the initial tasting of a whisky some regular tasters like to add a drop or two (but not much more) of water to the liquid in the glass and sniff it again. It's amazing what a difference this can make. That small quantity of water reacts with the alcohol to release more of the aromas and can sometimes give quite a marked difference from the first impression.

Finally, never say things like: 'I don't like the taste of whisky'. With so many hundreds – maybe even thousands – of different whiskies on the market it is highly unlikely that there is not a single one that appeals to your taste buds. So it's probably not a matter of not liking whisky at all. You have, most probably, simply not yet found the one that suits your palate.

whisky areas

Scotland

Many drinkers refer to whisky generically as 'Scotch' and, while this is not strictly correct, it is not surprising as Scotland produces a vast range of whiskies that differ widely in style, flavour and price.

Scotland is divided into several whisky regions, each of which produces whiskies in its own distinctive style. The reason for the differences lies in factors such as the quality of the peat, which is used in the drying fires, and the water, which forms the basis of the distilling process and often flows across peat bogs before reaching the distillery.

The Highlands, for example, are the craggy, windswept areas to the far north. Speyside, also in the north of Scotland, is known for the waters of the River Spey and its tributaries that bring the purest water from the lochs. One of these tributaries is called the Livet, home of the famous Glenlivet brand. The area is known for its mellow flavours and subtle peatiness.

The Lowlands, which surround Edinburgh, have a comparatively sunny, dry climate and are said to produce the best barley in Europe.

The island of Islay produces the most heavily peated whiskies, pungent and full of robust flavour. These include the legendary Lagavulin whisky.

The Western Highlands, include the Isle of Skye, the Mull of Kintyre (home of Campbeltown malts), Orkney and Jura. Whiskies from this region are usually heavily smoky in character. Skye is the home of the famous Talisker single malt whisky.

The most fashionable whiskies from Scotland are the 'single malt' whiskies, produced only in pot-stills and from a single distillery.

Most of the products of the

distilleries are blended to make the famous brand names like Johnny Walker, Bells, Ballantine, Haig and White Horse.

The length of maturation also makes a difference to the flavour (and cost) of a whisky. As it ages, the spirit absorbs more of the warm oak flavours. Obviously whisky that is maturing represents capital tied up in stock, and is therefore increasingly expensive as it ages. The age stated on the label of a Scotch whisky is that of the youngest component of a blend. A five-year-old blend may well contain whisky that is older than five years, for example. Once it is bottled a whisky does not age further. If you buy a 12-year-old whisky and keep it for three years, that doesn't make it a 15-year-old whisky.

Ireland

The Irish have been making whiskey for much longer that the Scots. Irish whiskey production can be traced right back to the reign of King

An Irishman is the only person in the world who would step over a dozen naked women to get to a bottle of booze.

Anon

James I, and the first whiskey was produced in the north-east corner of the island, where the land was good for growing grain, the water was pure and there was plenty of peat, all adding up to ideal whiskey-producing country along the shores of the Bush River. King James granted a licence to produce whiskey in about 1608 and the Bushmills distillery was started. Amazingly, it is still in production today.

Most Irish whiskey is triple distilled, so the resulting spirit is quite neutral in character until it has been aged in sherry or bourbon casks. Today Ireland produces more than 20 different brands of whiskey. The Irish developed the continuous still method of producing alcohol, which is used more widely today in

Scotland for the production of big-volume blends. Well-known Irish whiskeys include brands like Jameson, Tullamore and Bushmill's. Jameson's was judged the best whiskey in the world in Chicago in 1996.

It was largely through the efforts of immigrant Irish people that the American whiskey industry grew. This probably accounts for the similarity in spelling. The Irish brought that 'e' with them.

America

Whiskey distilling was brought to America by Irish and Scottish immigrants, with the Irish in the majority (in the early eighteenth century a quarter of a million struggling Irish people left the harsh conditions of their island and set off to seek a brighter future in America).

Many of these Irish immigrants followed the westward trail across the continent, looking for good farming land, and found it in areas like Pennsylvania, Virginia and the Carolinas. Later part of Virginia was turned into the state of Kentucky with a sizeable Irish population already settled in it.

Rye was a crop that flourished in these areas and it was not long before the Irish were producing what was to become one of America's favourite drinks – rye whiskey. Another grain in plentiful supply was maize, (called 'corn' in America) and this is used today in the production of bourbon and Kentucky whiskeys. Rye is also used in some brands, such as Jack Daniels and Jim Beam. (Incidentally, a whiskey can only be called 'bourbon' if it is made from at least 51% of corn, or maize.)

Jack Daniel was one of the most famous of all America whiskey distillers. Known as 'Little Jack' because of his tiny stature, he founded his distillery near

pages 20–21: Locke's Distillery Museum in Kilbeggan, Ireland

Lynchburg in Tennessee in 1866. Today the products of that company still bear the motto: 'Whiskey made as our fathers made it'. The statue of Jack Daniel in the grounds of the famous distillery is claimed to be the most photographed landmark in all of Tennessee.

Many of America's leaders owed their living to whiskey. George Washington grew rye at Mount Vernon; Abraham Lincoln worked for a distiller in his youth and General Ulysses Grant had a reputation of being a hard drinker. Richard Nixon is said to have drowned his Watergate woes in copious glasses of rye whiskey, while the powerful Kennedy family obtained their wealth from the distribution of liquor during the prohibition years.

During the American Civil War liquor peddlers travelled between military camps, illegally selling whiskey to the thirsty soldiers. They carried their stocks in bottles tucked into their top boots, giving them the

below: Federal troops drinking whiskey during the American Civil War

nickname, 'bootleggers'. With the introduction of Prohibition in 1919 bootlegging took on a sinister aspect and gave rise to the violent gangs that made fortunes from distributing illegal booze. This was the age of Al 'Scarface' Capone, 'Legs' Diamond and Lucky Luciano. Many lives were lost in the violent turf battles between the liquor-running gangsters. Because of the scarcity of legal alcoholic drinks during Prohibition, a whole industry of moonshine distilling grew up, often producing liquor of unspeakably poor – and sometimes downright toxic – quality. Much of this was passed off as genuine Irish Whiskey, and the drink developed rather a bad reputation as a result. These illicit spirits also contributed to the popularity of the cocktail. They really did need something added to them to make them bearable.

It took many years for the Irish whiskeys of America to regain their lost reputation, by which time the Canadian industry had gained a firm foothold on the North American market.

Canada

Canada's whisky production (without the 'e') received a big boost when America introduced Prohibition in 1919. Huge volumes of Canadian whisky were smuggled into the USA and brands such as Seagrams and Crown Royal were well established on the world market by the time prohibition was lifted in 1933. At one stage at the height of Canada's whisky production there were as many as two hundred distillers in the country. Today there are probably less than a dozen. One of them, Seagrams, has grown to be one of the world's most successful liquor companies. Other brands of note from Canada

I am not a heavy drinker. I can sometimes go for hours without touching a drop.

Noel Coward

23

include Royal Crown, Canadian Club, Black Velvet and Lord Calvert.

Canadian whisky is made from cereal grains, such as corn (maize) rye, barley and wheat and most are blended whiskies. The process used for Canadian whisky is much the same as that used elsewhere, and Canadian law requires whisky to be aged in casks for at least three years, although many of them are given a much longer maturation.

Japan

While not as widely known for its whiskies as Scotland, Ireland and North America, Japan is in fact the second biggest producer of single malt whiskies in the world.

Japan's official whiskey history starts in 1924, shortly after the great Kanto Earthquake destroyed Tokyo and Yokohama. Shinjiro Torii, a pharmaceutical wholesaler, bought a piece of land near Osaka and built the Yamazaki Distillery, founding what has now grown into a prosperous industry. There are

about 10 whiskey distilleries in modern Japan, most of them owned by three big distilling companies, Suntory, Nikka and Kirin.

The Japanese whiskey industry began as a deliberate effort to copy the style of Scotch whiskies, and they obviously became experts at doing that. Most Japanese whiskey is consumed locally and for many years it was generally believed to be inferior to the products of the old established Scottish and Irish distilleries. Recently, however, blind tastings have produced some surprises and Japanese whiskeys have achieved scores as high as – and on some occasions, higher than – some of Scotland's most revered products.

Whisky lovers all over the world are discovering that good Japanese whiskeys are worth adding to their collections. Once the Japanese whiskey producers get their marketing into top gear the rest of the world had better prepare for fierce competition.

for peat's sake!

Scottish whisky distillers will tell you that peat plays a vital role in the character of their famous products. Just as the chalky soils of the Champagne region of France contribute to the clean fresh character of Champagne, so peat is the 'terroir' of the great Scottish malt whiskies.

The mountain streams that feed the distilleries are filtered through layers of aromatic peat, giving the water the perfect flavour. This peat stream water is used to steep the grains of barley and cause them to sprout in the malting process. Obviously the character of the water becomes part of the individual flavour of the malt. The peat itself is also cut into blocks, dried and burned to dry the malt. This gives it the distinctive smoky character for which many of the whiskies are famous. If you can find a small piece of peat, light it and smell the wisp of pale blue smoke it emits. Remember that warm aroma. You will meet it again and again when you taste fine malt whiskies.

What is peat?

Peat is, in fact, an embryonic form of coal, consisting of semi-fossilised plant material – mainly a moss called 'sphagnum' – that has decomposed over many millennia to form a dark, chocolate brown, clay-like substance.

The layer of peat in the bogs of Scotland and Ireland are about

above: Peat blocks at an Irish distillery

a metre (3 feet) deep and are usually cut (or 'cast') in May each year to allow plenty of time for the summer sun to dry out the peat blocks before they are needed for fuel in the following winter.

Before the peat is cut the surface layer of moss is removed using a spade-like instrument called a cabar-lar to reveal the solid peat below. This is then dug out into brick-shaped blocks with another specialised tool called a torr-sgian and the blocks are stacked upright in threes or fours and left to dry.

Dried peat has been used as domestic fuel in many countries and is valued for its fragrant pale blue smoke, which gives the house a warm, rich fragrance similar to that which is so highly valued in good Scotch whisky.

Peat has played a vital role in the lives of countless generations of Gaelic folk so it is not surprising to learn that peat bogs were regarded as home to many gods and spirits in prehistoric times. Peat cutters (and more recently archaeologists)

My grandmother is over eighty and still doesn't need glasses – just drinks straight out of the bottle.

Henny Youngman

often find ritual objects buried deep in the peat, probably placed there during the bronze and iron ages as offerings to the spirits. Most puzzling of these offerings are wooden containers of a hard animal fat, known as 'bog butter.' It is not known for certain whether these caches of bog-butter were buried to preserve them or as an offering to the local spirits. Offerings of jewellery, weapons and bronze artefacts have also been found buried in the peat bogs.

Through its vital role in whisky, peat definitely forms a strong link between the modern drinker and his ancestors.

whisky tales

> **I feel sorry for people who don't drink. When they wake up in the morning, that's as good as they're going to feel all day.**
>
> Frank Sinatra

The world of whisky is rich with stories of the colourful characters who built the industry.

Raising the spirits

Magnus Eunson, founder of the Highland Park Distillery in the eighteenth century, was a respected verger (called a Beadle in those days) of his church by day, and a sly smuggler by night. In his book, Whisky Distilleries of the United Kingdom, Alfred Barnard describes a typical incident involving the wily Eunson.

Hearing that a new team of customs men was about to search his church for illicit liquor, Eunson quickly moved the kegs to his house and lined them up in the middle of an empty room, where he covered them with a board and a clean white cloth.

The officers searched the church, and when they found nothing illegal they set off for the house. Eunson gathered his people around the draped barrels, which looked very like a funeral bier, and as the excise men entered, the 'congregation' set up a mournful wailing and weeping. Kneeling at the head of the 'coffin' and clutching his Bible, Eunson signalled to the excise officers that there had been a death and one of the 'mourners' whispered 'small-pox' to the senior official. Nobody with any sense stayed around when there was smallpox in the area, so the officer and his men left as quickly as they could, leaving the mourners in peace.

Bombs away!

During America's Prohibition years the smuggling of liquor became a huge industry and many ingenious ways were devised to transport booze across the country's borders. As with all illicit substances, the prices of liquor soared to great heights, making smuggling enormously profitable.

The country's long coastline made it almost impossible to patrol it effectively, so smugglers developed ingenious techniques to bring their wares ashore. It was brought into the country in garbage barges, sponge-diving vessels and anything else that floated and would not attract the attention of the US Coast Guard.

One of the most imaginative of these ventures was used on the notorious schooner, Rosie. She carried an 'arsenal' of torpedoes, each about 5 metres (16 feet) long. These were filled with Scotch malt liquor and each had an air chamber on top to ensure they floated just below the surface of the water. The torpedoes could be towed close to the shore and released at pre-arranged spots, to be picked up by shore parties.

Speedy spirits

The Prohibition era gave rise to a typically American hobby, which continues to be popular to this day – customising cars.

After the moonshiners had produced the illegal liquor in their stills hidden deep in the woods, they then had to transport it to their customers in the cities. This could be a hazardous journey. Very often the police and excisemen knew of these stills but did not dare approach them for fear of being shot at. Instead they lay in wait on the roadside to catch the vehicles heading city-wards with their illegal cargoes.

The smugglers soon realised they needed vehicles which would out-run the Law. Part of the trick, of course, was to increase the speed and efficiency without attracting attention to the vehicle.

A whole industry sprang up to increase the power and speed of the moonshine vehicles so they would be able to beat the cops in a race. From the outside they remained innocent-looking family sedan cars, but they had enormous engines squeezed under their hoods. Roof-lines were lowered to reduce wind resistance and make the cars less conspicuous, and interiors were stripped out to reduce weight (and provide extra cargo space).

Today customised car shows attract millions of vehicle enthusiasts across America. It all started with liquor.

Medical aid

One of the few ways in which American citizens could obtain alcohol legally during Prohibition was by having a doctor prescribe it 'for medicinal purposes.'

Apparently many doctors grew very wealthy from writing out suitable prescriptions for their ailing patients. Maybe the modern world would be a happier and more peaceful place if the national health services of various countries prescribed a course of good alcohol for their citizens.

Whisky is by far the most popular of all the remedies that won't cure a cold.

Jerry Vale

a toast!

When we drink, we get drunk. When we get drunk, we fall asleep. When we fall asleep, we commit no sin. When we commit no sin, we go to heaven. So, let's all get drunk and go to heaven!

Brian O'Rourke

No matter where we live on the planet, or how informal the occasion may be, we almost always feel the urge to say some special word or words when we drink. Regular drinkers find it almost impossible to fill a glass and start slurping away without some small pause – some micro-ceremony – dedicating the drink to somebody's health, or to friendship, or simply to life.

Traditionally sailors drank a toast to mark the beginning – and end – of a long sea voyage, and many of them would pour a small libation overboard as a thank you offering to Neptune (or Poseidon, as the case may be). Even the lonely drunk slouched at the bar will raise his unsteady glass to the barman and say: 'Cheers', before taking the first mouthful.

This custom probably has its roots in the days when alcohol was revered for its medicinal and health-giving properties. It was the 'water of life' and one doesn't partake of those waters without some degree of reverence or ritual.

The drinking of toasts is a universal habit and every country has its own special word or words to use. Here are some that might be useful for the travelling imbiber to learn:

Australia, Britain and in most former British colonies: *'Cheers!'*

China and Japan: *'Kampei!'*

Denmark, Norway, Sweden: *'Skal!'*

Finland: *'Kippis!'* (Cheers)

France: *'Santé!'* (Health)

Germany: *'Prosit!'* (Your health)

Greece: *'Stin ygia sou!'* Usually

shortened to 'yassu!' and meaning 'Health!')

Ireland and Scotland: *'Slainthe!'*

Israel: *'L'Chaim'* (To life!)

Italy: *'Cin-cin!'* (Good things)

South Africa: *'Gesondheid!'* (Health)

Spain and Mexico: *'Salud.'*

Poland and Russia: *'Na Zdrovye!'* (Your health)

Yugoslavia: *'Zivelli!'*

Of course, there are many other traditional toasts that are drunk at more formal occasions, such as a toast to a bride and groom, or the formal toast to launch a ship, celebrate a victory or simply to start the drinking at a formal dinner.

Some are almost poetic and have become traditional at special occasions. The Irish have a most moving traditional toast:

'May the road rise up to meet you.
May the wind be always at your back.
May the sun shine warm upon your face.
And the rains fall soft upon your field.

And until we meet again
May God hold you in the palm, of His hand.'

A less wordy, but still cheering and saucy toast goes:

'May you live as long as you want to,
And want to as long as you live'.

Some of the rather puzzling toasts that are often heard include:

'Here's mud in you eye.' (Why?)

And the mind-bending Scottish toast:

'Here's to you, as good as you are,
And here's to me, as bad as I am,
And as bad as I am, and as good as you are,
I'm as good as you are, as bad as I am.' (Huh?)

Rather less confusing is another traditional toast which goes simply:

'Here's to your enemies' enemies.'

I once heard a grumpy old man raise his glass and say to his companion *'Here's to us and others like us'*. His equally grumpy pal replied solemnly, *'Damn few, and they're all dead.'*

Cheers!

the mourning after

**Drink because you are happy,
and never because you are miserable.**

G.K. Chesterton

In my Dictionary of Drink I find the definition of a hangover given as 'indisposition due to a heavy bout of drinking.' Which is rather like describing World War 2 as 'a spot of bother' or the flooding of New Orleans as a 'bit of damp.'

Most of us who take our drinking seriously have experienced at least one whopper of a hangover and vowed henceforth never to touch another drop.

But we always do. Mankind is slow to learn.

There can be few afflictions quite as dreadful as a full-blooded hangover. Your dried brains rattle painfully against the sharp edges inside your skull and your tongue tastes as though a small animal died in your mouth a month ago. The horror is that you can't spit it out because you just know the rest of you will follow it if you do.

You're afraid to get up from your bed because you know the action will cause violent motion sickness. Indisposition? Hah!

Whole books have been written on hangover cures, few of which actually work. Humorist Robert Benchley was pretty close to the mark when he said 'The only real cure for a hangover is death.'

But there are a few ways in which to reduce the suffering. The obvious one, which the sufferer probably wants to do anyway, without any persuasion, is to stay in bed with the curtains tightly drawn until it all goes away. Apparently vitamin B and C helps to detoxify the liver, but who has vitamins handy in desperate times like these?

Experienced drinkers know that when it comes to a hangover, prevention is far better than cure. This does mean, more or less, that you have to plan your hangover in advance. One good rule is to drink plenty of water during your imbibing session. Alcohol is a diuretic and the drying out of the system is a major part of a hangover's agony. (Coffee is also a diuretic, so don't think a strong coffee will improve matters). My Jewish friends assure me that chicken soup helps to prevent hangovers too. Apparently it replaces lost liquid and coats the stomach lining with a protective layer of schmaltz. If they are to be believed, chicken soup will also cure everything from flu to a broken heart.

A glass of milk before you start drinking will slow down your alcohol absorption. I am reliably informed that a slice of bread thickly buttered should be eaten before a party. Apparently the butter adds a protective coating to the stomach lining.

Fructose helps to burn up alcohol, and bread is quite a good source of fructose. A slice or two during the evening might reduce the chances of a bad hangover, or at least soften the agony.

Fresh fruit juice is another good source of fructose.

A paracetamol tablet taken with plenty of water before going to bed is often helpful. But it's not much use once you've developed the hangover. It has to be taken before you sleep. I have great faith in this preventative measure, but it may just be the glass of water that does the trick. Still, I'm convinced it has saved me from many mournful mornings.

The real answer, of course, is to drink in moderation so the problem doesn't arise. However, I know – and you know – that this advice is unlikely to find universal favour. For some of us, hangovers are as inevitable as death or taxes. We have no option but to pay our dues and accept them as a tax on what has gone before.

Since bottled mineral water has become fashionable it is quite acceptable to drink a glass of

> **When I read about the evils of drinking, I gave up reading.**
>
> Henny Youngman

mineral water for each glass of alcoholic beverage you consume. Apparently that helps too.

Some hardened drinkers offer truly horrendous 'cures' involving Worcestershire sauce, raw eggs, pepper and other unspeakable ingredients. One such concoction is known in America as a 'Prairie Oyster.' You'll find recipes for it in many books on drinks. The only benefit I can see from this is that it will probably empty your stomach very rapidly and rather messily. Nobody with a real hangover could look a raw egg in the eye and live.

why 'cocktail'?

Everybody has a theory about how mixed drinks became known as 'cocktails'. The truth is that nobody knows for certain but the name has been in use for more than a century and a half. There are dozens of explanations of the word's origin, some so far-fetched that they could possibly even be true. One could fill a whole book with stories claiming to tell of the true origin of cocktails. Whether they are fact or fiction, they're worth re-telling, because a good story is always valuable entertainment.

French-speaking drinkers have a theory that a French chemist in New Orleans used to serve tiny, strong drinks in egg-cups. The French word for an egg-cup is 'coquetier', so they were referred to as 'coquetiers', which soon became changed to 'cocktails'.

One of the best known of the theories is that of Betsy Flanagan, the barmaid and widow of a French revolutionary soldier. She used to steal roosters from a neighbour who was unsympathetic to the cause, in order to feed revolutionaries who came to her tavern.

Her drinks were often decorated with the colourful tail feathers of these stolen fowl as a gesture of defiance, and her loyal customers used to raise a glass and drink a cheeky toast to 'Vive le cock-tail'.

My favourite version of the cocktail story is a little known one about the American Army unit that had been involved in several skirmishes with King Axolotl of Mexico in the nineteenth century. Eventually a truce meeting was called in an effort to make peace. When the representatives of both sides were seated in the royal hall, the Mexican king offered the American general a drink. A young serving wench was summoned and entered carrying just a single cup. An embarrassed silence fell over the assembled meeting, because they all realised that no matter whether the king or the general was offered the drink first, the other would be deeply offended. The young lady quickly assessed the situation, bowed respectfully and drank the drink herself. The general was so impressed that he asked her name. It was Coctel. And so the general named mixed drinks after the quick-thinking maiden.

Another story from the American War of Independence claimed that Squire Allen, who was a regular customer at the Bunch of Grapes Inn, once lost his favourite fighting cock and was heart-broken. After a while a young officer came riding into town with the missing rooster safely tucked under his arm. The squire was so grateful that he ordered the barmaid, Daisy, to provide the man with the finest drink in the house. She mixed a wonderful concoction and they all drank a grateful toast to the 'cock's tail', which had not lost a single feather during its bid for freedom.

Fighting cocks feature in many of the cocktail legends. One version claims that fighting cocks were given a powerful potion to drink in order to boost their courage and aggressiveness before being put into the cock-pit. The drink, naturally, was known as 'cock-ale', and each cock owner had his own secret recipe. The owners apparently drank a similar mixed drink to celebrate when their valiant birds won a fight (or to drown their sorrows when they lost).

No doubt you have your own favourite story about the origin of the word.

making cocktails

> **And when the ball was over,**
> **Everyone confessed**
> **They all enjoyed the dancing,**
> **But the drinking was the best.**

Anon

Like so much that is associated with modern drinking habits, the cocktail party was one of the offshoots of the American Prohibition years between 1919 and 1933.

Firstly, some of the drinks produced illegally by the 'moonshiners' were so unspeakably dreadful that they could not possibly be enjoyed on their own. It was necessary to mask the horrible taste by adding fruit juices, sodas and fruit to the raw alcohol. This made cocktails not only fashionable, but essential. Those who made up the best recipes found themselves popular hosts.

Secondly, the Prohibition laws banned the sale and transportation of liquor, but it was still legal to drink any stocks you already had in your home. Those who were lucky enough (or devious enough) to have bottles of real booze (or even illicit alcoholic drinks) in their homes became popular hosts. They could invite their friends round to enjoy drinks in a relaxed (and legal) atmosphere without having to look over their shoulders from time to time to check whether the place was being raided.

They could 'speak easy'.

Clandestine bars trying to copy this relaxed atmosphere became known as 'speakeasies. '

This book aims to appeal to home hosts rather than professional bartenders. The idea is to help hosts and hostesses to create an easy atmosphere where friendly chat and good drinks are the order of the evening.

Equipping the bar

> **Sometimes too much drink is**
> **barely enough.**

Mark Twain

Whatever your hobby or interests, they are always more pleasurable when you have the right equipment. This applies equally to photography, woodwork, painting or embroidery – or even making cocktails.

A well-equipped cocktail bar is a delight to work in, and specialist bar stores stock an appealing array of odds and ends for mixing, straining, measuring and stirring. You could spend a fortune on fancy bar gadgets and appropriate décor items. On the other hand, if you serve cocktails only occasionally to a few close friends, you'll probably find most of the tools you need right in your kitchen.

A good cocktail shaker is a pleasure to use. It is designed to blend ingredients by beating them with ice cubes, and it has a spout with a built-in strainer, so you can pour the cocktail into a glass and leave the ice behind.

If you do not have a proper shaker, find an attractive screw-cap jar and an appropriate sized strainer.

You'll find that almost all cocktail recipes call for ice in one form or another. Always have plenty of ice available. It is used in a cocktail shaker for several reasons. It acts as a beater, to ensure a thorough blend of ingredients, it chills the drink and it dilutes it slightly. Also, no cocktail would be quite the same without that subtle tinkle of ice cubes against the sides of your glass.

An electric blender is useful for making a smooth drink out of semi-solid ingredients like fruit. Failing that, a food processor works quite well, and even a hand-whisk will do in some cases.

Proper bar measures are a pleasure to use, but your kitchen probably contains a range of measuring cups and spoons that will serve just as well. In any case, exact measurements are for pedants.

A tall glass jug or pitcher is often needed for mixing ingredients. You will probably own one already.

An ice bucket is also essential

equipment as almost all cocktails require plenty of ice but a plastic bowl will serve as a substitute. Ice tongs help to transfer ice from one container to another. A pasta spoon (the kind with fingers round the edge) makes quite a good ice carrier, and a tablespoon will also do the job at a pinch.

An electric ice crusher is useful for those recipes that call for crushed ice, but you can do a reasonable job of crushing ice by placing the ice cubes in a plastic bag and smacking them with a steak tenderising hammer – or whacking the bag against a convenient wall. Just make sure it's a strong bag. And a strong wall.

A selection of glasses is always good to have, whether for cocktails or straight drinks. Cocktails, however, are festive drinks and have more appeal if they are served in pretty glasses. Start a collection of fun glasses for parties. They do not necessarily need to match. Basically you need lowball glasses (or whisky glasses), highball glasses (or beer tumblers) and cocktail glasses (or wine goblets). Shot glasses are pretty for small drinks or chasers, but small sherry glasses will do if you do not have proper shot glasses.

A word about choosing glasses: they come in a wide range of prices, from elegant cut crystal to cheap and cheerful supermarket ranges. Unless you live in that rarified layer of society where only the very best will do, select inexpensive glasses for normal party use.

Accidents do happen, and if a guest happens to break one of your irreplaceable cut crystal goblets it will ruin his evening as well as yours, whereas a broken supermarket glass rates little more than a shrug and a 'don't worry'. There's the added factor that some expensive lead crystal goes milky when washed in a dishwashing machine. The cheap ones come up sparkling time after time.

A small bar towel is essential for wiping up spills and drying damp hands. A kitchen towel will do, but make sure it's a pretty one if you're making the drinks in front of your guests.

A long spoon is good for stirring ingredients together. Check your cutlery drawer. Proper bar spoons have a 'muddler' at one end of the handle. This is handy for jobs like crushing mint leaves with sugar in the bottom of a tankard.

Prepare

> **I distrust camels, and anyone else who can go for a week without a drink.**
>
> Joe E Lewis

Whether you're having a quiet drinks session with two or three close friends, or a more formal cocktail party for 50 guests, a little preparation makes all the difference between a successful, relaxed evening and a stressful failure.

Your guests want to see you and chat to you, so they don't enjoy having you disappear into the kitchen every few minutes to search for a strainer or find the ice bucket that is being used as a flower vase. Before the first guests arrive, do a quick check to ensure you have enough glasses, ice, water, mixers and equipment readily to hand. You should have a reasonable working surface too, with a bowl to hold spoons and tongs when they're not in use, and a cloth to wipe glasses and spills.

The traditional bar counter was evolved so the host could serve his guests while facing them. Some home drinks arrangements ensure the host spends most of the evening with his back rudely toward his guests. You may not have a home bar in your house, but it might be a good idea to arrange a small table for serving drinks, so you can stand behind it and chat to guests face-to-face while mixing their cocktails. Quite often a tea trolley will provide the ideal drinks dispensing surface, with the upper tray acting as a work surface and the lower on serving as a storage area for bottles and equipment.

One of the essentials of any cocktail bar is ice, more ice and even more ice. Tepid drinks are an abomination. Make sure you have a good supply of ice cubes before your party begins. There are shops that sell bags of ice cubes and they are not expensive. Buy several and keep them in your freezer, ready for use. You can never have too much ice. Any that's left over will be received gratefully by your houseplants.

Fruit juice

Fruit juices play an essential role in the making of cocktails. Wherever possible, try to use freshly squeezed juices, particularly when it comes to lemon juice. When this is not possible (maybe the particular fruit is not in season) you can use commercially made fruit juices. The fruit juice industry has improved enormously in recent years and in many cases it's hard to tell the commercial products from the freshly squeezed article.

Here again, preparation makes the difference. Try to have your fresh juice squeezed, stored in jugs and kept chilled well in advance of your first guests' arrival.

cocktail recipes

creating your perfect drink

Cocktail making (sometimes called mixology) is more an art than a science, although there are plenty of people who take it very seriously. In my opinion recipes should be regarded as guidelines rather than precise formulae. Everybody's tastes differ and what delights one drinker may well disgust another.

Every good bartender has his or her own style, and this is what makes some great and others merely good. The martini, for example, is the most widely known of all cocktails and consists basically of just two ingredients – gin and vermouth, but cocktail enthusiasts will travel halfway round the world to experience the legendary martini of some famous mixologist in New York, Chicago, Venice or Paris. Whole books have been written about the simple martini, which is obviously not as simple as it seems.

The quantities and proportions given in these recipes are for your guidance only. Do feel free to experiment with them, increasing a little here and reducing there until you find the taste that is exactly right for you.

Wherever possible we have used proportions rather than exact measures. Where a recipe says 'one part of whisky to two parts of vermouth', it doesn't matter whether you use a teaspoon or a bucket as the measure, as long as the proportions remain the same. One reason for doing this is that bar measures differ from country to country. Some use 'jiggers' or 'tots' while others use fluid ounces and yet others prefer to list their ingredients in millilitres. Some people refer to a shot glass and others know it as a 'pony'.

You may enjoy finding the particular kind of whisky that is exactly right for your version of the Manhattan or the Rob Roy. But whiskies (and whiskeys) come in such a vast range of flavours and styles that it would be enormously expensive to try to collect them all. For the purpose of stocking your cocktail bar it is probably fine to keep one blended Scotch and one bourbon or rye whiskey. Of course, if you can afford a wider range of whiskies you'll have a wider range of flavours with which to experiment.

A Canadian or Japanese whisky could produce a very different cocktail to the one using a blended Scotch.

Balance is vital

The secret of any good drink lies in the balance between the various flavour components. Sweetness on its own can be cloying and boring, but when it is balanced by a touch of acidity it becomes exciting. In good beer the bitterness of the hops is balanced by the comfortable sweetness of the malt.

The best selling soft drink in the world, Coca-Cola, is popular because it enjoys a fine balance between sweetness and acidity. It quenches a thirst and leaves the palate feeling clean and fresh. A good cocktail should do the same.

When designing a cocktail use lemon or lime juice to add a clean sourness or acidity to the flavour, but balance it with something slightly sweet, like sugar syrup or a sweet liqueur like Galliano.

There are several brands of bitters on the market and a few drops of any of these can be used to sharpen the character of an otherwise bland drink.

There are five basic flavours that go to make up the whole range of taste experience. These are sweet, sour, bitter, salty and savoury (otherwise known as 'umami'). Experiment with combinations of these, always looking for the perfect balance.

Sense and silliness in the Decor

Many cocktail recipes call for garnishes or decoration. These can serve several purposes. Ideally, a drink should appeal to all the senses. It should taste good (of course) but it should also smell good, look good and even sound good (hear those ice cubes tinkling in the glass?).

A drink should look appealing, so a bright red maraschino cherry will add a festive touch to an otherwise plain looking drink. The garnish might also add flavour, particularly in the case of lemon slices or twists. It can also add a scent, as in the case of crushed mint leaves. Some drinks have pieces of fruit floating in them, to serve as decoration as well as flavour.

Avoid silly artificial decorations like paper umbrellas and plastic swizzle sticks in the form of naked women. They have no place in a really good cocktail and are often used simply to distract attention from an otherwise dull drink.

While purists might throw up their hands in shock and horror at the thought of using anything as precious as Scotch whisky in a cocktail, It does blend well with other flavours and hundreds of fine cocktails have whisky as their base. There are those, however, that have a specifically Irish character, and it's best to stick to an Irish whiskey when making them, just as it's probably best to use a Bourbon whiskey in an American drink.

In most cases it's best to use a relatively inexpensive, commercial blended whisky as a cocktail ingredient. There's no point in giving your sensitive Scottish friends heart attacks by adding triple sec and a squeeze of lemon juice to your 12-year-old Glenlivet. Many liquor chain stores stock their own budget brands of whisky and these are just fine for cocktails, especially when you are experimenting with different proportions of ingredients and may find your first attempt not as pleasant as you hoped. South Africa produces a fine budget whisky called Three Ships, which is a blend of good quality Scotch whisky and locally made grain whisky matured in cask for a minimum of three years. Interestingly, it often scores highly in blind tastings, sometimes even out-pointing well-respected Scottish malts, much to the irritation of those who consider themselves connoisseurs.

Three Ships makes the perfect base for a cocktail.

scotch
old-fashioned

Purists may argue that a good whisky needs no additions, but this drink adds a little bitter-sweet touch that appeals to many drinkers.

A cube of sugar

A few dashes of Angostura bitters

Two bar measures of Scotch whisky

Ice cubes

Soak the sugar cube in angostura bitters and place it in the bottom of a lowball glass.

Add just enough water to dissolve the sugar cube, then pour in the whisky. Stir gently and add two or three ice cubes.

boston flip

A flip is basically a drink that includes the raw yolk of an egg and is said to be a great health drink – or a cure for a hangover. Modern drinkers will probably balk at the thought of swallowing anything with raw egg in it, but the truth is it's rather a pleasant little drink. The risk of salmonella is probably very slight.

Ice cubes

One part bourbon whiskey

One part sweet fortified wine (Madeira if you have it)

One egg yolk

A dash of gomme syrup

Grated nutmeg

Place five or six ice cubes in a cocktail shaker and add the whiskey, Madeira, egg yolk and gomme syrup. Shake very well for at least 10 seconds and strain it into a chilled cocktail glass. Grate a little nutmeg over it and serve.

cablegram cocktail

Before the high-speed communication offered by e-mail and mobile phones, the cablegram was considered a miracle of technology. After centuries of having communications limited to the speed of a horse or sailing ship, you could suddenly send a message to somebody on the other side of the world – in less than a day! No wonder people celebrated this wonder by naming a cocktail in its honour.

Ice cubes

One generous part of rye whiskey

One teaspoon of sugar syrup

Juice of half a lemon

Ginger ale

Twist of lemon

Place three ice cubes in a cocktail shaker and add the whiskey, sugar syrup and lemon juice. Shake well and strain into a highball glass filled with ice cubes.

Top up with ginger ale and add a twist of lemon before serving.

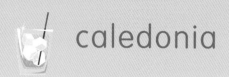

caledonia

This drink will appeal to whisky lovers. Glayva is a drink made of whisky with herbs and spices added, so what we're getting here is a double helping of whisky with all the trimmings.

Ice cubes

One part Scotch whisky

One part Glayva

Juice of one lemon

A dash of grenadine syrup

Half an egg white

Slice of lemon

Maraschino cherry

Place three or four ice cubes in a cocktail shaker and add the whisky, Glayva, lemon juice, grenadine syrup and egg white. Shake very well and strain into a chilled cocktail glass, decorate with the slice of lemon and cherry then serve.

california lemonade

This is a refreshing long drink to enjoy on a sunny Californian summer's day. Don't be fooled by the name – or the straw. It's still a grown-up drink.

Crushed ice

One part bourbon whiskey

The juice of one lemon

Two teaspoons of caster sugar

A dash of grenadine

Soda water

Slice of orange

Slice of lemon

Maraschino cherry

Place a scoop of crushed ice in a cocktail shaker and add the whiskey, lemon juice, sugar and grenadine. Shake well and strain into a tall glass half filled with crushed ice. Top up with soda water and decorate with the orange, lemon and cherry and serve with a straw.

comfortable screw

The name of this drink is probably derived from a screwdriver, which is basically vodka and orange juice. We replace the vodka with Southern Comfort liqueur here, hence the comfortable name. While not strictly a whiskey-based cocktail, it comes close enough, as Southern Comfort is based on whiskey.

Ice cubes

One part Southern Comfort

Six parts fresh orange juice

Banana pieces

Place six ice cubes in a cocktail shaker and add the Southern Comfort and orange juice. Shake well and strain into a lowball glass. Float a couple of pieces of banana on top, and serve.

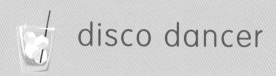

disco dancer

We have no idea why this drink was called a disco dancer. Maybe it will have you dancing on the table, or possibly it inspired a disc jockey to reach new heights.

Ice cubes

Two parts blended Scotch whisky

Two parts peach brandy

Six parts fresh orange juice

A dash of grenadine

Half an egg white

Slice of orange

Place four ice cubes in a cocktail shaker and add the whisky, peach brandy, orange juice, grenadine and egg white. Shake very vigorously and strain into a highball glass. Decorate with a slice of orange and serve.

forester's delight

The blue curaçao gives this drink a mysteriously green colour, which is probably why it delighted a forester. It will probably give you just as much delight.

Crushed ice

One part bourbon whiskey

One part Cointreau

Two dashes of blue curaçao

A dash of lemon juice

Caster sugar

Place a scoop of crushed ice in a cocktail shaker and add the whiskey, Cointreau, curaçao and lemon juice. Shake well. Frost the rim of a cocktail glass with caster sugar and strain the drink into it, and serve.

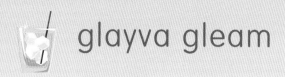

glayva gleam

While Glayva may not be strictly classed as a whisky, it is a drink that consists of whisky with herbs and spices added, so we feel justified in including it here. In any case, it's a pretty little drink that's stood the test of time.

Ice cubes

Half an egg white

Two parts Glayva

One part orange curaçao

A dash of lemon juice

Twist of lemon (optional)

Place four ice cubes in a cocktail shaker and add the egg white, Glayva, orange curaçao and lemon juice. Shake very well, strain into a chilled cocktail glass and serve ungarnished. If you think it looks a bit plain you can add a twist of lemon.

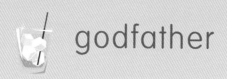# godfather

The history of liquor is spiced with tales of gangsters and violence. It seems the human race regards alcoholic drinks so highly that we are prepared to kill for it. Godfathers used to be kindly souls who looked after our religious wellbeing. More recently they have gained a rather more sinister reputation. Let's hope this drink was named after the old kind of godfather.

Ice cubes

Two parts Scotch whisky

One part Amaretto

Fill a lowball glass with ice cubes, pour the whisky over it, followed by the Amaretto. Stir very gently and serve.

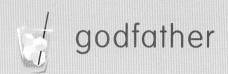

godfather

The history of liquor is spiced with tales of gangsters and violence. It seems the human race regards alcoholic drinks so highly that we are prepared to kill for it. Godfathers used to be kindly souls who looked after our religious wellbeing. More recently they have gained a rather more sinister reputation. Let's hope this drink was named after the old kind of godfather.

Ice cubes

Two parts Scotch whisky

One part Amaretto

Fill a lowball glass with ice cubes, pour the whisky over it, followed by the Amaretto. Stir very gently and serve.

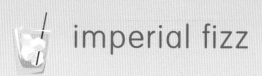

imperial fizz

This is a pleasantly refreshing tall drink to enjoy while watching a game of polo from the veranda of the clubhouse. Or simply any time that you happen to be thirsty.

Ice cubes

Two parts Scotch whisky

One part Bacardi rum

The juice of half a lemon

Soda water

Place three or four ice cubes in a cocktail shaker and add the whisky, rum and lemon juice. Shake well, strain into a highball glass and top up with chilled soda water before serving.

trois rivières

This delightful drink comes from Canada and its English name is Three Rivers. To experience it at its best you should use a Canadian whisky as the base.

Ice cubes

Two parts of Canadian whisky

One part Dubonnet

One part triple sec

Place four or five ice cubes in a cocktail shaker and add the whisky, Dubonnet and triple sec.

Shake well and strain into a lowball glass and serve ungarnished.

hoots mon

This unusual drink uses Lillet, which is a French aperitif made of wine, fortified with Armagnac and flavoured with a selection of herbs and fruit, as a mixer. Strangely enough its flavours blend well with those of a blended Scotch whisky.

Ice cubes

Two parts Scotch whisky

One part Lillet

One part sweet vermouth

Twist of lemon

Place three cubes of ice in a cocktail shaker and add the whisky, Lillet and sweet vermouth. Shake well and strain into a chilled cocktail glass. Squeeze the lemon over the drink and drop it in before serving.

horse's neck

Some books of cocktail recipes claim that a horse's neck should be made with brandy, while others say only whisky makes the 'real thing.' Whichever you choose, it's a pleasant thirst quencher.

Ice cubes

One part Scotch whisky

Six parts ginger ale

Slice of lemon

Place two ice cubes in a highball glass, pour the whisky over them, then top up with ginger ale. Squeeze over the lemon slice and drop it in before serving.

ink street

One can't help wondering where this old classical cocktail got its name. Our guess it that it was dreamed up by a journalist, and possibly in Fleet Street, where the printer's ink flows around the clock.

Ice cubes

One part rye whiskey

One part fresh orange juice

One part fresh lemon juice

Place two or three ice cubes in a mixing glass and add the whiskey, orange juice and lemon juice. Stir well, strain into a lowball glass and add two ice cubes before serving.

irish blackthorn

The blackthorn is a bush with hard, dark wood, often used for the making of stout walking sticks. It also produces sloe berries, used in the production of sloe gin. It's rather strange then that this cocktail uses no gin, but is based on Irish whiskey.

One part Irish whiskey

About two-thirds as much dry vermouth

Three dashes of Pernod

Three dashes of Angostura bitters

Ice cubes

Stir all the ingredients together thoroughly in a mixing glass. Fill a lowball glass with ice cubes and pour the mixed ingredients over them and serve.

irish shillelagh

This drink should more logically be called the Blackthorn, because it contains sloe gin, which comes from the blackthorn berry, but the previous recipe must have beaten it to the name. However, my old dictionary defines a shillelagh as 'An Irish cudgel of blackthorn or oak,' so it all makes some sort of Irish sense after all.

Ice cubes

One part Irish whiskey

One part sloe gin

Half a part of dark rum

A dash of gomme syrup

Juice of half a lemon

Pieces of soft fruits (whatever is in season)

Place four ice cubes in a cocktail shaker and add the whiskey, sloe gin, rum, gomme syrup and lemon juice. Shake thoroughly and strain into a lowball glass. Decorate with neat pieces of fruit and serve.

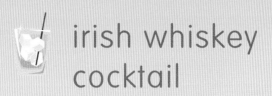

irish whiskey cocktail

This is one of those recipes that just asks for experimentation. By changing the proportions of the ingredients you can create a whole range of different flavours.

Ice cubes

One part Irish whiskey

A splash of Pernod

A splash of Cointreau

A dash of Maraschino

A dash of Angostura bitters

Green olive

Place four ice cubes in a cocktail shaker and all the ingredients except the olive. Shake well and strain into a chilled cocktail glass. Drop in the green olive and serve.

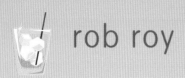

rob roy

This drink, named after the famous Scottish hero, was designed to be raised as a toast whenever great heroes are honoured.

Ice cubes

Two dashes of Angostura bitters

One generous part of Scotch whisky

One equally generous part of sweet vermouth

Piece of orange peel

Place two ice cubes in a lowball glass and splash in two dashes of Angostura bitters.

Add the whisky and vermouth, squeeze the orange peel over the drink to release the zest and drop it into the glass. Stir once gently and serve.

scots dream

To make this drink in the proper manner, the recipe calls specifically for an Islay malt whisky – not just any old Scotch. The Islay malts are known for their robust peat aroma and it is probably this assertive character that gives the drink its unique flavour.

Crushed ice

One part Islay malt whisky

A dash of fresh lime juice

One teaspoon of thick cream

Place a scoop of crushed ice in a mixing glass and add the whisky and lime juice. Stir well and strain into a chilled cocktail glass. Carefully float a layer of thick cream on top and serve.

seaboard cocktail

The seaboard is traditionally the boundary between the sea and the land. A friend who tasted this cocktail at the end of a long hard drinking session declared it to be the boundary between seasick and homesick. Pay him no heed. He was not himself at the time. It's actually very pleasant.

Ice cubes

One part bourbon whiskey

One part gin

One part fresh lemon juice

A splash of gomme syrup

Sprig of mint

Place four or five ice cubes in a cocktail shaker, add the whisky, gin, lemon juice and gomme syrup and shake well. Strain into an ice-filled highball glass, decorate with the sprig of mint and serve.

serpent's tooth

Logic tells us this must be an extremely ancient recipe, because St Patrick drove all the snakes out of Ireland, so this must pre-date the good saint. Or maybe the last serpent to leave Ireland shed a tooth as it slithered into the sea and some canny Irish barman used it as a swizzle stick. (Any drink is improved by a good story.)

Crushed ice

Two parts Irish whiskey

One part Kummel

Two parts fresh lemon juice

Three parts sweet vermouth

A dash of Angostura bitters

Place a scoop of crushed ice in a mixing glass or bar pitcher and add the whiskey, Kummel, lemon juice, sweet vermouth and bitters.

Stir until all the ingredients are well mixed, then strain into a chilled wine goblet and serve.

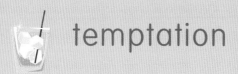

temptation

There have been several cocktails with the name Temptation, each one based on some sort of whisky or whiskey. Having tried three (more would have been greedy), we settled for this rather delicious tall drink.

Ice cubes

Two parts Scotch whisky

One part orange liqueur

Juice of half a lemon

A dash of grenadine

Orange juice

Slice of orange

Place four or five ice cubes in a cocktail shaker and add the whisky, orange liqueur, lemon juice and grenadine. Shake well and strain into a highball glass filled with ice cubes. Top up with chilled orange juice and decorate with a slice of orange, slit and slipped over the rim of the glass, and serve.

tennessee sunrise

This drink, which gets its name from the glowing colour, should obviously be made with rye whiskey for authenticity. Bourbon serves as a suitable substitute. You can balance the flavours by adjusting the acidity with lime juice and the sweetness with the maraschino.

One part rye whiskey

A generous splash of maraschino

A dash of fresh lime juice (to taste)

Ice cubes

Stir the whiskey, maraschino and lime juice together in a lowball glass. Fill with ice cubes and stir again gently before serving.

the waldorf

Traditionally Bourbon whiskey is used in this classic American cocktail, but you can experience a whole range of flavours by using different whiskies.

Crushed ice

Two parts Bourbon whiskey

One part Pernod

One part sweet vermouth

A dash of Angostura bitters

Place a scoop of crushed ice in a bar glass and add the Bourbon, Pernod, vermouth and bitters.

Stir well and strain into a chilled cocktail glass. Serve ungarnished.

thunderclap

This is a seriously strong cocktail that should not be taken too fast. It is sometimes served almost in the form of a challenge. 'I bet I can make you something that will knock your socks off!'

Ice cubes

One part bourbon whiskey

One part dry gin

One part brandy

Place four ice cubes in a cocktail shaker and add all three ingredients. Shake well and strain into a chilled cocktail glass and serve.

irish coffee

The Irish have long been in the habit of adding a small dash of whiskey to their tea. It is believed that this variation was invented by American airmen serving at Shannon Air Force Base during World War II. Americans have always preferred coffee to tea.

One part Irish whiskey

Five parts strong black coffee

A teaspoon of brown sugar

One part thick cream

Pinch of chocolate powder (optional)

Pour the Irish whiskey and hot coffee into an Irish coffee glass (basically a goblet with a handle to prevent you burning your fingers). Add sugar to taste and stir until it is dissolved.

Using your steady hand, trickle the thick cream over the back of a spoon on to the coffee, so it floats on the surface. The mark of a good Irish coffee maker is the clean, straight dividing line between the coffee and the cream.

You may wish to sprinkle a pinch of chocolate powder onto the cream as garnish.

the irish handshake

This merry little Irish cocktail is as fine a way as any of welcoming a guest to your home. Of course it requires an Irish whiskey to give it the proper friendly character.

Ice cubes

Two parts Irish whiskey

One part green curaçao

One part fresh cream

Place four or five ice cubes in a cocktail shaker, add all the ingredients and shake well. Strain into a chilled cocktail glass and serve.

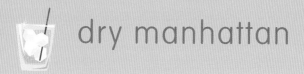

dry manhattan

One of the popular modern versions of the Manhattan is the Dry Manhattan, which is basically the same as the original Manhattan, with dry vermouth substituted for the sweet vermouth.

You'll need all the ingredients listed for the Manhattan, substituting dry for sweet Vermouth.

Crushed ice

Three parts whiskey (preferably a blended rye whiskey)

One part dry vermouth

A dash of Angostura bitters

Maraschino cherry

Fill a mixing glass with crushed ice, add the whiskey, vermouth and dash of bitters and stir well.

Strain into a cocktail glass or tall Champagne flute and garnish with the cherry before serving.

 affinity

This classic cocktail was popular in the 1920s and could probably be considered a slightly more complex version of the Manhattan.

Ice cubes

One part Scotch whisky

One part dry vermouth

One part sweet vermouth

A dash of angostura bitters

Twist of lemon

Place four or five ice cubes in a cocktail shaker and add the whisky and both vermouths. Add the dash of bitters and shake well. Strain into a chilled cocktail glass and squeeze the lemon twist over the drink to release the zest, but do not drop it in. Serve.

night owl

This is a drink that was designed to be served when the city was asleep and the music was mellow.

A dash of Angostura bitters

Cracked ice

Four parts Bourbon whiskey

One part lemon juice

One part triple sec

Chilled soda water

Splash a few drops of bitters into a highball glass and swirl it about to coat the inside. Fill the glass with cracked ice.

Add the whiskey, lemon juice and triple sec and stir gently.

Top up with soda water and stir again, ever so gently.

Raise your glass to the rising sun and take the first sip to toast the new day.

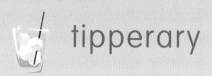

tipperary

Traditionally the Irish serve green beer on St Patrick's Day, so why not mark the event with a green whiskey instead?

Ice cubes

One part Irish whiskey

One part sweet vermouth

Half a part of green chartreuse

Place four or five ice cubes in a cocktail shaker, add all the ingredients and shake well.

Strain into a cocktail glass and serve.

new yorker

This elegant drink provides the perfect opportunity of experimenting with the right balance between sweet and sour flavours. Why not make several, adjusting the quantities of lime juice and sugar syrup in each until you find the one that suits your palate perfectly.

Crushed ice

Three parts Scotch whisky

One part fresh lime juice

A teaspoon (or more) of sugar syrup

A dash of grenadine

Twist of orange peel

Place a scoop of crushed ice in a cocktail shaker and add the whisky, lime juice, sugar syrup and grenadine. Shake well and strain into a chilled cocktail glass. Squeeze the orange peel over it and drop it in as garnish before serving.

whisky mac

This very simple drink has become a classic. It is also said to be an excellent remedy for a cold. But why wait for a cold?

Crushed ice

One part Scotch whisky

One part ginger wine

Place a scoop of crushed ice in a cocktail shaker and add the whisky and ginger wine.

Shake well and strain into a cocktail glass. Serve ungarnished.

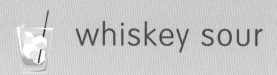

whiskey sour

The sour has been a popular drink from as long ago as the 1850s. It was originally made with Cognac, but any spirit will do well. The most popular sour today is undoubtedly the whiskey sour.

Ice cubes

Two parts bourbon whiskey

One part fresh lemon juice

A dash of gomme syrup

Maraschino cherry

Place five ice cubes in a cocktail shaker and add the whiskey, lemon juice and gomme syrup. Shake vigorously and strain into a chilled cocktail glass.

Garnish with the maraschino cherry and serve.

scotch mist

This could be regarded as the Scottish equivalent of the Irish coffee. Originally a Scotch Mist was simply Scotch on the rocks with a twist of lemon zest over it. This is probably the English version. It's a nice little warmer for a chilly winter's day.

One part Scotch whisky

Three parts freshly brewed strong tea

Honey

Thick cream

Mix the whisky and tea together and add honey to taste. Stir well and pour into small (demitasse) coffee cups. Float a teaspoon of thick cream on the surface and serve.

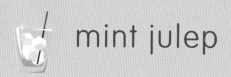

mint julep

The mint julep was the traditional drink of wealthy Southern plantation owners in America. Not many people today can afford a 'tankard of bourbon whiskey,' but there are times when you might like to live like a millionaire for a day.

Crushed ice

A tankard of bourbon whiskey

A teaspoon of caster sugar

Two tablespoons of water

One teaspoon of Barbados rum

A bunch of freshly picked mint leaves

Ice cubes

Place a cup of crushed ice in a pitcher and add the bourbon, caster sugar, water and rum. Stir well.

Place the mint leaves in a serving jug and crush lightly to release the flavour.

Strain the contents of the pitcher into the jug containing the mint, add a few ice cubes and serve in lowball glasses, garnished with one or two of the mint leaves.

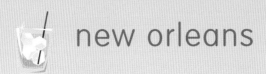

new orleans

This cocktail evokes visions of Dixieland jazz and the Mardi Gras in a city that will probably never be the same again. Serve it as a tribute to a great bygone age.

Crushed ice

Three parts bourbon whiskey

One part Pernod

Three dashes of Angostura bitters

One dash of anisette

A teaspoon of sugar syrup (or to taste)

Ice cubes

Twist of lemon

Place a scoop of crushed ice in a cocktail shaker and add the bourbon, Pernod, bitters, anisette and sugar syrup. Shake well and strain into a lowball glass filled with ice cubes. Garnish with a twist of lemon and serve.

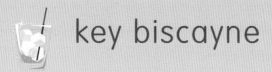

key biscayne

This typically American cocktail will probably taste best with an American bourbon or rye whiskey. If you don't have one available, any whiskey will do.

Crushed ice

Three parts whiskey

One part curaçao

One part sweet vermouth

Juice of half a lime

Sprig of mint

Place a scoop of crushed ice in a cocktail shaker and add the whiskey, curaçao, vermouth and lime juice. Shake well and strain into a chilled cocktail glass.

Garnish with a sprig of mint, lightly crushed, and serve.

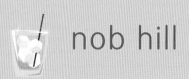

nob hill

The secret of any drink is in the balance. This one allows you to experiment with the balance between the sour/bitter grapefruit and the sweet honey until you find the proportions exactly suited to your palate.

Ice cubes

Two parts rye whiskey

One part grapefruit juice

Honey to taste

Place four or five ice cubes in a cocktail shaker and add all the other ingredients.

Shake very well and strain into a chilled cocktail glass. Serve ungarnished.

martha washington

It doesn't really matter whether Martha Washington ever drank this cocktail. It's just a good way of keeping her name alive.

Crushed ice

Two parts Rye or bourbon whiskey

One part cherry liqueur

A splash of lemon juice

One teaspoon of sugar syrup

Maraschino cherry

If you have a blender, place a scoop of crushed ice in it and add all the other liquid ingredients. Blend until smooth, strain into a chilled cocktail glass and decorate with the cherry.

If you do not have a blender shake the ingredients together in a cocktail shaker.

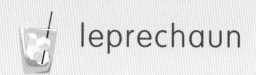

leprechaun

The Irish say if you catch a leprechaun he will grant you one wish in exchange for his freedom. Maybe this delicious drink was made up to compensate for a failed leprechaun hunt.

Ice cubes

One part Irish whiskey

Two parts tonic water

Lemon peel

Place three ice cubes in a tall glass and pour the whiskey and tonic water over them. Squeeze the lemon peel over the drink and drop it in. Stir very gently and serve.

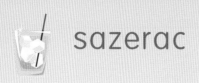

sazerac

This drink got its intriguing name from a French company that imported brandy from France, Sazerac du Forge et Fils. Later rye whiskey replaced brandy in the recipe, but the drink retained its name. Quantities are vague, so it's the perfect recipe for experimentation.

A sugar cube

A dash of Angostura bitters

Ice cubes

Two generous measures of rye whiskey

A splash of Pernod

Twist of lemon

Soak the sugar cube in Angostura bitters and place it in a chilled lowball glass with an ice cube.

Add the whiskey and stir well. Splash in the Pernod, twist the lemon over it and drop it in. Serve.

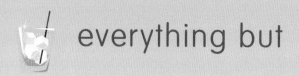

everything but

In this timid age we live in, some drinkers may balk at the thought of including a raw egg in a drink. If that's you, ignore it and go on to something safer. For those who like to live dangerously, however, it's a delicious experience.

Ice cubes

One part rye whiskey

One part dry gin

One part orange juice

One part lemon juice

Half a part of apricot brandy

A teaspoon of caster sugar (or to taste)

One raw egg

Place five or six ice cubes in a cocktail shaker and add the whiskey, gin, orange and lemon juice, apricot brandy, sugar and egg.

Shake vigorously until it is smooth and velvety and strain into a highball glass. If you really want to make it a memorable experience, frost the rim of the glass before using by dipping it in some egg white and then into caster sugar.

depth charge

This is related to the Boilermaker, the difference lies in the way it is served. A boilermaker is simply a mixture of beer and whisky. The depth change packs an exciting taste explosion.

A shot glass of blended whisky

A bottle of chilled lager beer

Fill the shot glass with whisky and place it carefully in the bottom of a beer tankard, glass and all. Carefully fill the tankard with beer, trying not to upset the shot glass.

When the drinker tilts the tankard to drink, the shot glass falls over, trickling the whisky down the side. Instead of getting one blended taste, you have the two drinks reaching your tongue separately.

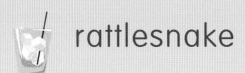

rattlesnake

This drink probably earned its name in the Prohibition days in America, when the rough moonshine liquor was sometimes known as 'snake juice.' This version is far more civilised.

Crushed ice

Two measures of Bourbon whiskey

Several dashes of Pernod

One teaspoon of lemon juice

One teaspoon of sugar syrup

Half an egg white

Place a scoop of crushed ice in a cocktail shaker and add all the ingredients. Shake vigorously for at least 20 seconds, then strain it into a chilled lowball glass and serve. An attractive white froth should form on the surface.

lady hunt

This elegant cocktail was named after Lady Caroline Hunt, founder of the Rosewood Hotels. It blends several compatible flavours together in a delightfully mellow combination.

Ice cubes

Three parts whisky

One part Tia Maria

One part Amaretto

The juice of half a lemon

Half an egg white

Slice of orange

Maraschino cherry

Place four or five ice cubes in a shaker and add all the liquid ingredients, including the egg white. Shake vigorously and strain into a chilled cocktail glass.

Decorate with the orange slice and cherry, and serve.

rusty nail

This is a simple drink which blends two quite similar flavours, as Drambuie is a whisky-based liqueur. A harmonious result is almost guaranteed.

Two parts Scotch whisky

One part Drambuie

Ice cubes

Twist of lemon

Pour the whisky and Drambuie into a lowball glass, drop in two ice cubes, stir gently and garnish with the twist of lemon before serving.

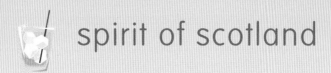

spirit of scotland

Only a good blended Scotch will do in this very Scottish drink. Drambuie, of course, is made of whisky, heather and honey. What could be more Scottish? This is a slightly more tangy version of the Rusty Nail, from the previous page.

Crushed ice

Two parts Scotch whisky

One part Drambuie

Juice of half a lemon

Place a scoop of crushed ice in a blender (or a cocktail shaker if you do not have a blender) and add all the ingredients.

Blend well (or shake vigorously) and strain into a chilled cocktail glass.

clubman cocktail

This is not strictly a whiskey-based cocktail, but Irish Mist is a liqueur made from Irish whiskey flavoured with honey and herbs, so it has been included. It's a very colourful drink.

Ice cubes

One part Irish Mist

Four parts orange juice

Half an egg white

A dash of blue curaçao

Place four or five ice cubes in a cocktail shaker and add the Irish Mist, orange juice and egg white.

Shake vigorously and strain into a lowball glass. Carefully trickle drops of blue curacao down the sides of the glass to add delicate lines of colour, and serve.

dom pedro

Nobody seems to know who Dom Pedro was or how this delightful after-dinner drink got his name, but it's appearing on more and more South African restaurant menus. Sometimes it is offered as a pudding, rather than a drink.

Soft vanilla ice cream

A generous measure of whisky (you can also use Kahlua for variation)

Chocolate vermicelli

Almost fill a lowball glass with soft vanilla ice cream and pour a generous measure of whisky over it.

Whip it thoroughly with a fork until the two are well blended, sprinkle the chocolate vermicelli on top and serve. A long spoon is usually offered to reach those last lurking drops.

old fashioned

This quite simple drink has been around since about 1900 and has the distinction of having a Cole Porter song named after it: 'Make it Another Old Fashioned, Please.'

A sugar cube

A dash of Angostura bitters

Soda water

A generous measure of bourbon whiskey

Twist of lemon

Slice of orange

Maraschino cherry

Place the sugar cube in a tall glass and soak it with the Angostura bitters and a few drops of soda water. Crush the sugar with the back of a bar spoon, add the whiskey and fill the glass with soda.

Squeeze in the twist of lemon and orange and then garnish with the cherry.

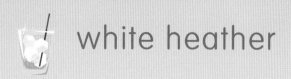# white heather

This delicious cocktail was the winner at an international bartender's competition. The creator, Rodney Brock, specified the brands of each ingredient, but we leave it to readers to use whatever they have available.

Ice cubes

One part Scotch whisky

One part crème de banane

One part crème de cacao

Two parts single cream

Grated nutmeg

Place four ice cubes in a cocktail shaker and add all the ingredients except the nutmeg. Shake well and strain into a cocktail glass. Grate a little nutmeg over it and serve.

whisky fix

This cheerful drink is designed to clear the head and revive the spirits after a long hard day's work.

Crushed ice

Two parts blended Scotch whisky

One part fresh lemon juice

Caster sugar

Small pieces of fresh peach (or any other soft fruit that's in season)

Fill a lowball glass with crushed ice and add the whisky, lemon juice and sugar. Stir well and garnish with a few small pieces of fresh fruit. Serve.

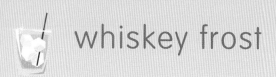

whiskey frost

This is a refreshing drink that requires a little preparation time well before your party. Fill an ice tray with fresh lemon juice and freeze it into cubes ready for use.

Ice cubes

One part bourbon whiskey

One part medium cream sherry

One part port

A dash of sugar syrup

Two cubes of frozen lemon juice

Slice of lemon

Place four ice cubes in a cocktail shaker and add the bourbon, sherry, port and sugar syrup.

Shake well and strain into a lowball glass. Add two cubes of frozen lemon juice and garnish with a slice of lemon over the rim of the glass before serving.

four-leafed clover

This decidedly Irish drink would obviously be best when made with Irish whiskey. The green colour makes it ideal for serving on St Patrick's Day.

Crushed ice

One part Irish whiskey

One part crème de menthe

One part thick cream

Maraschino cherry

Place a scoop of crushed ice in a cocktail shaker and add all the ingredients except the cherry.

Shake well and strain into a cocktail glass. Garnish with the cherry on a cocktail stick and serve.

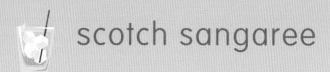

scotch sangaree

This recipe calls for heather honey, but any honey will do at a pinch. It makes a refreshing tall drink.

Heather honey (ideally)

A generous measure of Scotch whisky

Twist of lemon

Ice cubes

Soda water

Grated nutmeg

Dissolve a dessertspoon of honey in a little water in a highball glass. Splash in the whisky and add the twist of lemon and three ice cubes. Stir gently and top up with soda water. Sprinkle a pinch of nutmeg over it and serve.

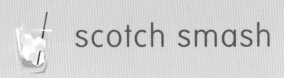

scotch smash

Here's a drink with a delightfully fresh aroma and flavour.

Six mint leaves

A dessertspoon of honey

Crushed ice

A generous splash of Scotch whisky

A dash of orange bitters

Place five mint leaves in a highball glass, add the honey and muddle the two together with the back of a spoon. Now fill the glass with crushed ice and add the whisky. Stir well, garnish with the remaining mint leaf and a dash of orange bitters and serve.

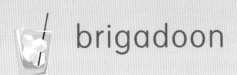

brigadoon

Here's a cheerful and tangy little drink to serve on a summer evening beside the misty loch.

Crushed ice

One part Scotch whisky

One part fresh grapefruit juice

One part dry vermouth

Ice cubes

Place a scoop of crushed ice in a blender or cocktail shaker and add all the ingredients. Blend well (or shake vigorously) and strain into a cocktail glass filled with ice cubes and serve.

loch ness

No book of whisky recipes would be complete without acknowledging Scotland's most famous resident, the Loch Ness monster. Here's the drink to raise in its honour.

Crushed ice

Two parts Scotch whisky

One part Pernod

Half a part of sweet vermouth

Place a scoop of crushed ice in a cocktail shaker and add all the ingredients. Shake well and strain into a cocktail glass and serve ungarnished.

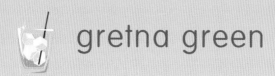

gretna green

Tradition has it that runaway lovers headed for Gretna Green to be married in haste before an angry father could stop the ceremony. Maybe this sweet-and-sour drink is an appropriate toast to marriage in general.

Cracked ice

Three parts Scotch whisky

One part heather honey

Two parts lemon juice

A splash of green Chartreuse

Place a scoop of cracked ice in a cocktail shaker and add all the ingredients. Shake very well until all the honey is dissolved. Strain into a chilled cocktail glass and serve.

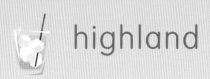

highland

This drink is reputed to be a soothing nightcap that ensures a good night's sleep. You may enjoy it so much you stay up for a second helping.

Crushed ice

One part Scotch whisky

Two parts full cream milk

One teaspoon of caster sugar

Grated nutmeg

Place a scoop of crushed ice in a cocktail shaker (or blender) and add all the ingredients except the nutmeg. Shake well and strain into a highball glass. Grate a little nutmeg over it and serve.

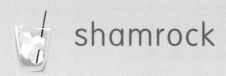

shamrock

There are several versions of the Shamrock, some of which use cream or ice cream, while the purists prefer whiskey and crème de menthe un-creamed. We prefer the one with thick cream for a really decadent drink.

Crushed ice

One part Irish whiskey

One part crème de menthe

One part thick cream

Ice cubes

Maraschino cherry

Place a scoop of crushed ice in a cocktail shaker and add all the ingredients except the cherry. Shake well and strain into a lowball glass, add ice cubes and garnish with the cherry before serving.

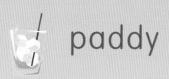

paddy

Paddy is the embodiment of an innocent Irish soul, free of guile and ready to please. This drink takes just a moment to prepare.

Crushed ice

Two parts Irish whiskey

One part sweet Vermouth

A dash of Angostura bitters

Place a scoop of crushed ice in a cocktail shaker, add all the ingredients, shake well and strain into a cocktail glass. Serve un-garnished.

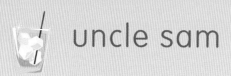 # uncle sam

This patriotic drink would not be the same with anything other than a good Bourbon whiskey as its base.

Ice cubes

One part bourbon whiskey

One part peach liqueur

Twist of lemon

Place four ice cubes in a lowball glass, add the bourbon and peach liqueur and stir gently. Squeeze the lemon twist over it to release the zest and drop it in before serving.

southern ginger cocktail

This is a comfortable cocktail rather like the 'horse's neck' much favoured by brandy drinkers. It can be made as a tall drink to enjoy on a hot summer's day, or as a shorter cocktail to serve as an aperitif before dinner.

Ice cubes

Two parts bourbon whiskey

One part lemon juice

Ginger ale

Twist of lemon

Place three or four ice cubes in a highball glass (or lowball glass for a shorter drink), add the bourbon and lemon juice and stir gently. Top up with ginger ale and garnish with a twist of lemon before serving.

happy horse

This drink, of course, is named after the White Horse whisky that forms its base. Purists may shudder, but it's actually very refreshing.

Ice cubes

One part White Horse whisky

Two parts fresh grapefruit juice

A dash of grenadine

Half an egg white

Slice of orange

Place four ice cubes in a cocktail shaker and add all the ingredients except the orange slice. Shake well and strain into a wine goblet. Decorate with a slice of orange before serving.

irish cheer

Several whiskey based cocktails include sweet vermouth as one of the ingredients. Cocktail makers have obviously discovered over the years that these two drinks are comfortable companions.

Ice cubes

Four parts Irish whiskey

One part sweet Vermouth

Slice of orange

Place three ice cubes in a lowball glass, add the whiskey and sweet vermouth and stir gently before decorating with a slice of orange slipped over the rim of the glass, and serving.

seven and seven

A drink that became popular among American servicemen before and during World War 2 was a highball consisting of Seagrams Seven Crown Canadian whisky and the fizzy drink called 7-Up. The name was a natural combination of the two ingredients.

Ice cubes

One part Seagrams Seven Crown Whisky

Five parts 7-up (or Sprite)

Place three ice cubes in a highball glass, add the whisky and 7-Up and stir gently before serving.

hot scotch toddy

Traditionally a hot toddy is made to relieve the misery of a cold. This one is thought to be so good that it is often used to prevent a cold. Prevention, they say, is better than cure, and you just never know when a cold might strike. Better be safe…

Three measures of boiling water

A teaspoon of honey

Two generous measures of Scotch whisky

The juice of half a lemon

Three dashes of Angostura bitters

Three cloves

Twist of lemon

Use a heatproof glass with a handle, like those used for making Irish coffee, and pour in the boiling water and honey. Stir to dissolve the honey and add the whisky, lemon juice and bitters. Now stick the three cloves into the twist of lemon and drop it into the drink before serving.

index